TEN H   ES

TEN HOUSES

Michael J. Crosbie

Alfredo De Vido | Architects

Rockport Publishers, Inc.
Gloucester, Massachusetts
Distributed by North Light Books,
Cincinnati, Ohio

First published in the United States of America by:

Rockport Publishers, Inc., 33 Commercial Street, Gloucester, Massachusetts 01930-5089

Telephone: (978) 282-9590, Fax: (978) 283-2742

Distributed to the book trade and art trade in the United States by:

North Light Books, an imprint of F&W Publications, 1507 Dana Avenue, Cincinnati, Ohio 45207

Telephone: (800) 289-0963

ISBN 1-56496-409-4

10 9 8 7 6 5 4 3 2 1

Cover Photograph: Moore House/Norman McGrath

Printed in Hong Kong by Midas Printing Limited

Graphic Design: Lucas H. Guerra / Oscar Riera Ojeda

Layout: Argus Visual Communication, Boston

Contents

Foreword

by Richard J. Wertheimer

On a summer weekend in 1982, when we drove to the Delaware shore to visit old friends who had just purchased a lot for their new beach house, we did not intend to retain master architect Alfredo De Vido. By the end of the weekend, however, Loretta and I surprised ourselves and astonished others by purchasing a nearby lot for a beach house of our own.

We retained Al De Vido the following weekend. We had known Al and Cathy socially and had admired the clean lines and efficient design of their East Hampton house. Around their pool that weekend, we talked to Al about our new house. I am certain he has heard none of this before: all we wanted were four bedrooms, fine ocean views, a couple of porches, modest construction cost, and low maintenance thereafter; we wanted no mansion-on-the-beach, but a good-looking design would not be unwelcome, thank you very much.

Al delivered all this and much more, as you will see (this page and section beginning on page 84). While there were, inevitably, a few small calls that we would make differently if starting again from scratch, we were well pleased with the house when it was finished. Al created a structure that is comfortable, functional, bright, easy and inexpensive to maintain, warmly welcoming, and beautifully integrated with the sand and salt water. The house is also elegantly proportioned and handsome inside, outside, and from inside out. Over the years, we and our family and friends have delighted in it.

I need not persuade any reader of this book that the best of architecture is fine art. Al De Vido created a work of art for us.

Hanging around with Al was also a treat. He was adept, thorough, well-organized, empathetic, practical, direct but gentle, as careful with my money as I am, and intellectually interested in almost everything. He even was interested in my law practice, and by the end of construction, he had become a formidable competitive threat to the licensed bar.

The author and I are pleased that Al stuck with architecture, and that he has delivered to other fortunate clients the considerable pleasures he bestowed upon us.

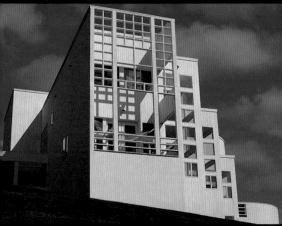

Introduction

by Michael J. Crosbie

Above: *View of the second-floor gallery of the De Vido House from the living room.*

Opposite Page: *The Moore House tucks into the hillside and has a grass-covered roof.*

At a time when much of the buzz in the architectural world is about globe-trotting architects and international commissions, it is easy to overlook another pattern of practice: that of the architect as a family practitioner, not unlike the local doctor. Alfredo De Vido is such an architect. Surely, he has not only designed houses in the confines of a single neighborhood or small town—the projects herein attest to a varied portfolio of buildings throughout the East Coast. But De Vido is a careful architect, paying close attention to context while freely interpreting it, arriving at solutions that always feel right for the circumstances. It is an approach to design and service that is disappearing, and all architects—especially young ones—can learn much from De Vido's work.

This book's foreword, by Richard Wertheimer—one of De Vido's enthusiastic clients—attests to the architect's care. Throughout the projects in this book you will not find unbridled ego and one-size-fits-all solutions. De Vido approaches each new house with a fresh eye, and all of these designs reveal an attention to the special needs of the client. Often, as in the Moore House, there is a sensitivity to siting and energy conservation that results in a seamless web of building and nature.

Another appealing quality of De Vido's architecture is its open-ended character. The buildings he creates seem easily added onto—we might call them organic. Perhaps the best example of this is his own house on Long Island, which grows (as if effortlessly) into the site, reaching out with walkways, pavilions, pools, and vegetation. Inside, the sun is always a welcomed guest. Many of his houses come alive with light, and De Vido's use of textured, natural materials resonate with the sun's grazing beams.

There is much intelligence in the way De Vido weaves the design of his houses with their construction. He has developed a modular technique that makes it easier for the builder to do a good job, and saves the client money at the same time. The houses are laid out on a 10-foot (3-meter) module, with inside spaces broken down into multiples or divisions of ten. Another modular dimension governs all vertical locations for floors, doors, and windows. This system results in houses that are easier to build and reduces job-site mistakes, without sacrificing unique design. It's just another example of the attention and care of one of architecture's outstanding family practitioners.

Moore House

Sharon, Connecticut

T he design for this house—on which the owners collaborated with the architect—included the goal of merging it with its natural environment. The site was selected for its beauty, and the house was designed to disturb it as little as possible. The house faces south toward a pond created by the owners, and the structure nestles into the hillside, fitting into the landscape with no exposure to the north. The house's passive-solar design features control the flow of energy through the building by natural means, utilizing energy-conservation principles.

The primary building material is concrete—sandblasted in some areas, faced with stone in others. Oak columns and beams lend a feeling of warmth. These materials are used both inside the house and outside in a harmonious arrangement.

Much consideration was given to the proportion of the walls and the balance of glass areas with the spaces behind them. Natural light spills into the north end of the house via a long row of skylights. Even on an overcast day, one does not feel "underground" in any room. The rich colors of the wood, stone, and other materials further forestall any sense of subterranean space.

Above: Viewed from the east, the house appears to become part of the site.

Opposite Page: From the southeast, the house opens to sunlight under its earth-covered roof.

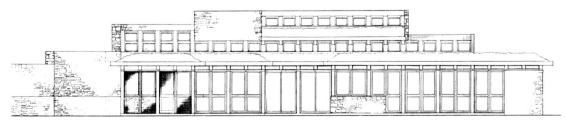

⊕ South

1. Entry
2. Master Bedroom
3. Guest Bedroom
4. Living Room
5. Kitchen
6. Dining Room
7. Studio
8. Porch

Floor Plan

Opposite Page: *Natural stone retaining walls with wood beams define the entry court and accentuate the living room.*

Right: *The quality of many of the spaces has a strong Japanese flavor.*

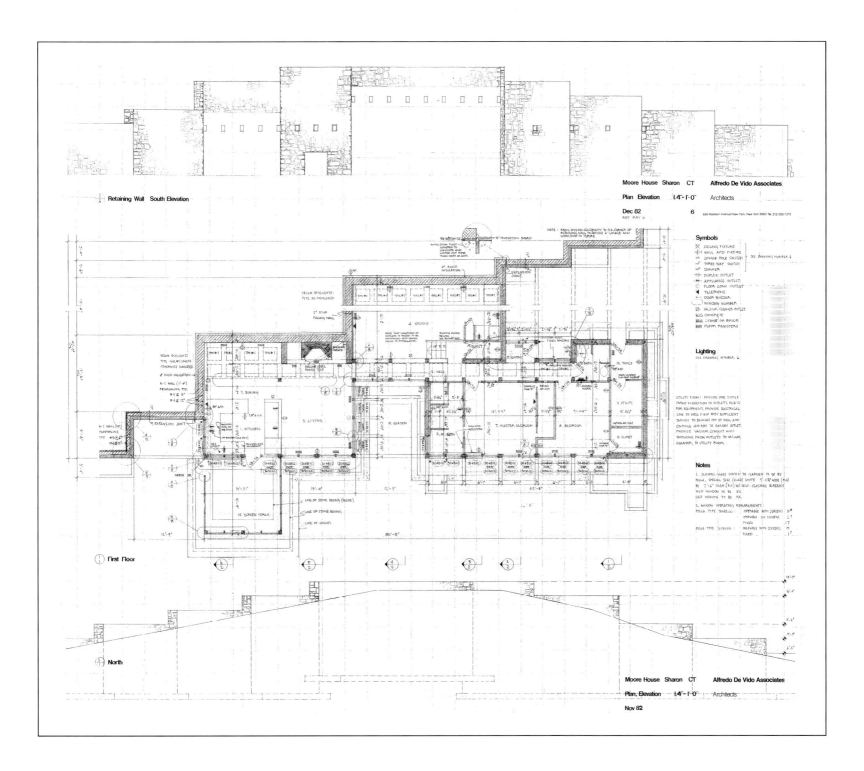

Retaining Wall South Elevation

Moore House Sharon CT   Alfredo De Vido Associates

Plan Elevation 1/4"=1'-0"   Architects

Dec 82
REV. MAY 6   6   699 Madison Avenue/New York, New York 10021 Tel. 212/355-7370

Symbols

⊠ CEILING FIXTURE
⊕ WALL MTD FIXTURE
S SINGLE POLE SWITCH
S₃ THREE-WAY SWITCH
S₀ DIMMER
⊖ DUPLEX OUTLET
⊟ APPLIANCE OUTLET
Ⓒ FLOOR CONN OUTLET
◁ TELEPHONE
⌒ DOOR CHIMES
○ WINDOW NUMBER
⊡ VACUUM CLEANER OUTLET
▨ CONCRETE
▨ STONE OR BRICK
▨ FLOOR REGISTERS

Lighting

SEE DRAWING NUMBER 6

Notes

1. SLIDING GLASS DOORS TO GARDEN TO BE BY PELLA, SPECIAL SIZE (CLAD) UNITS 9'-11½" WIDE (N.O.) BY 7'-6" HIGH (N.O.) W/ SELF-CLOSING SCREENS. WEST WINDOW TO BE XO. EAST WINDOW TO BE OX.

2. WINDOW OPERATING REQUIREMENTS:

First Floor

North

Moore House Sharon CT   Alfredo De Vido Associates

Plan, Elevation 1/4"=1'-0"   Architects

Nov 82

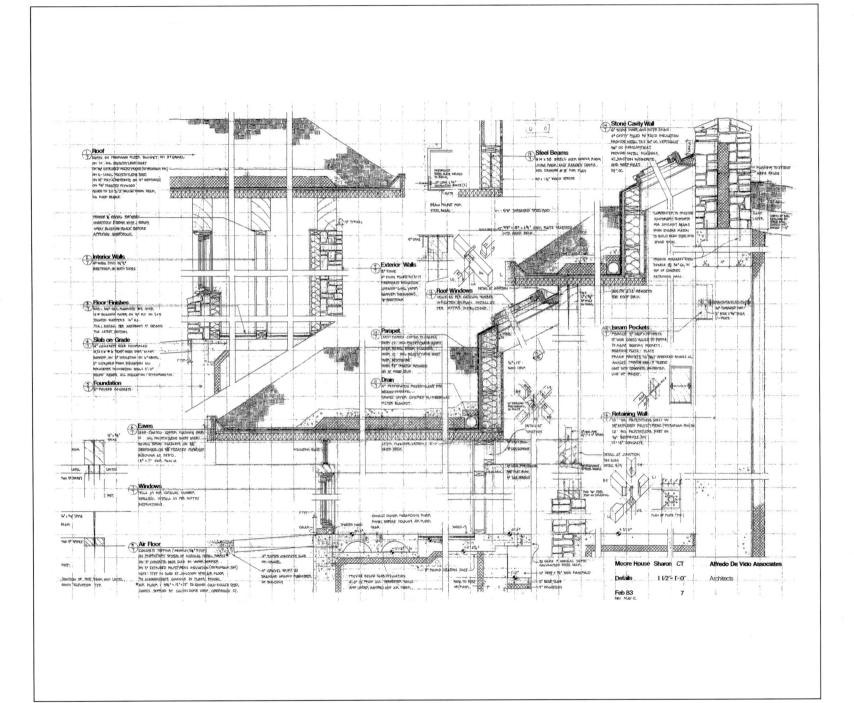

Moore House Sharon CT   Alfredo De Vido Associates

Details   1 1/2" = 1'-0"   Architects

Feb 83
REV MAR 15   7

Right: The massive stone fireplace is washed
with natural light from above.

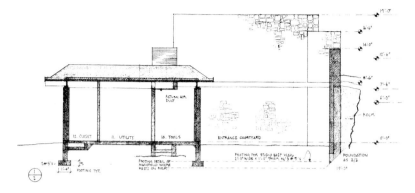

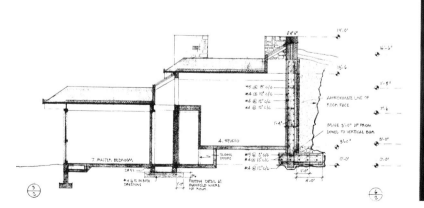

Left, top to bottom: Drawings and photographs demonstrate how natural light is introduced throughout this bermed house. Illumination is brought in through skylights, clerestories, and slivers of space, often washing walls of textured materials, or modulating the house's structure.

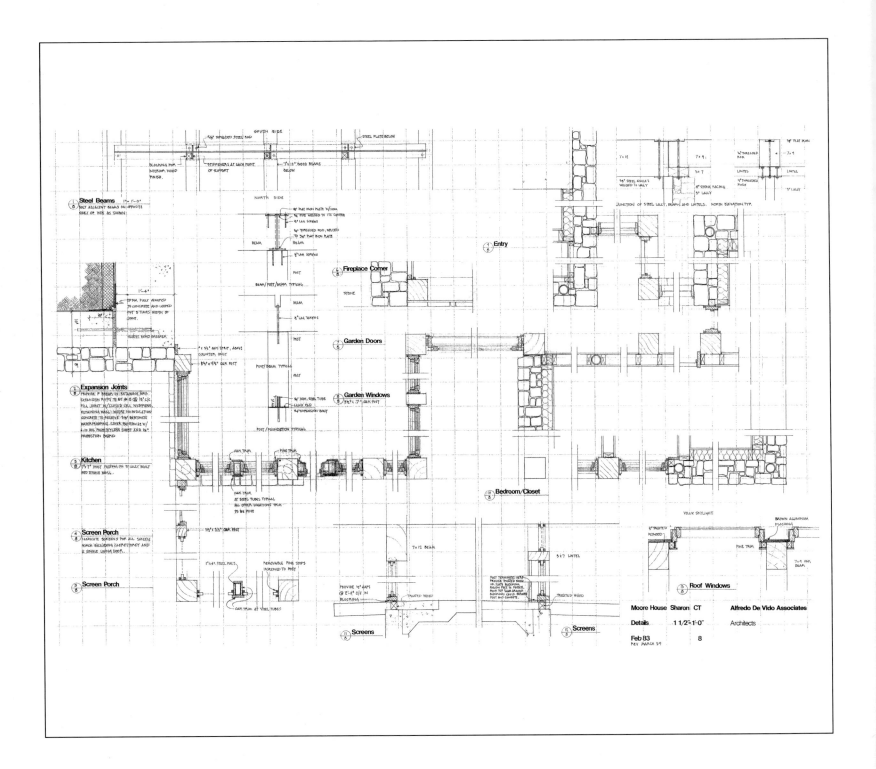

Moore House Sharon CT   Alfredo De Vido Associates

Details   1 1/2"=1'-0"   Architects

Feb 83   8
REV. MARCH 84

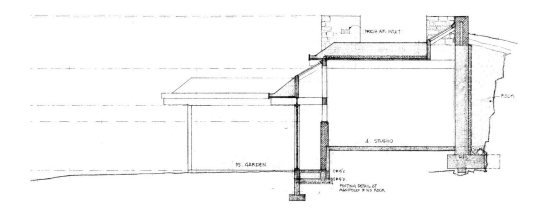

FRESH AIR INLET

ROCK

4. STUDIO

15. GARDEN

2#5's
2#5's
FOOTING DETAIL AT
MANIFOLD IF NO ROCK.

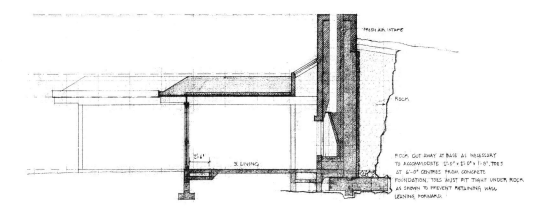

FRESH AIR INTAKE

ROCK

2'-6"

3. LIVING

ROCK CUT AWAY AT BASE AS NECESSARY
TO ACCOMMODATE 2'-0" X 2'-0" X 1'-8" TOES
AT 6'-0" CENTRES FROM CONCRETE
FOUNDATION. TOES MUST FIT TIGHT UNDER ROCK
AS SHOWN TO PREVENT RETAINING WALL
LEANING FORWARD.

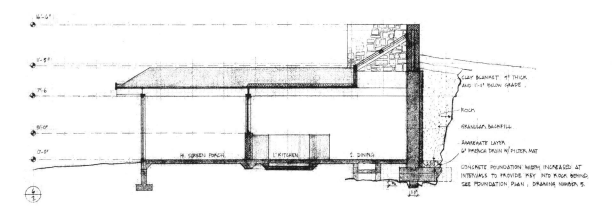

16'-6"

11'-5"

7'-6

2'-0"

0'-0"

4. SCREEN PORCH.

1. KITCHEN

2. DINING

CLAY BLANKET 9" THICK
AND 1'-0" BELOW GRADE.

ROCK

GRANULAR BACKFILL

AGGREGATE LAYER
6" FRENCH DRAIN W/ FILTER MAT

CONCRETE FOUNDATION WIDTH INCREASED AT
INTERVALS TO PROVIDE KEY INTO ROCK BEHIND,
SEE FOUNDATION PLAN, DRAWING NUMBER 5.

Wirth House

Waccabuc, New York

This three-level, 2,300-square-foot (207-square-meter) house is composed of strong rectangular forms distributed along a sloped site. Due to this arrangement of spaces, the house, when viewed from the steep maple and tulip tree lined drive, impresses one as a structure much larger than it actually is.

Thanks to the glazed openings to the north, the house gains generous views downhill. There are also high windows on the uphill, south side of the house to capture solar warmth during the winter. This north/south window arrangement also attracts prevailing summer breezes through cross-ventilation. This is aided by the flow of unimpeded spaces among the three levels.

The first floor, entered from the downhill side, contains three bedrooms. A flight of steps rises directly from the entry, leading to the dining room and kitchen. A few more steps ascend to the compact living room, with windows looking south, east, and west. Another flight leads to a study above the kitchen.

The design incorporates a stone retaining wall that runs along the slope. Natural materials are used throughout the house. Warm cedar boards on walls and floors combine with a tall fieldstone fireplace to provide an aura of solid comfort. The simple forms, warm rustic materials, and abundant light and views give this house a timeless quality.

Above: The uphill elevation of the house is more in keeping with the traditional scale of domestic architecture. Windows on these elevations capture south light and deliver it deep within the living spaces.

Opposite Page: Approaching the house from the driveway, the forms line up to create a variegated wall.

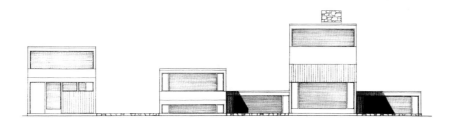

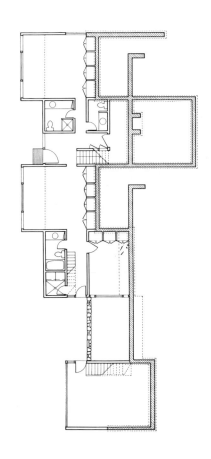

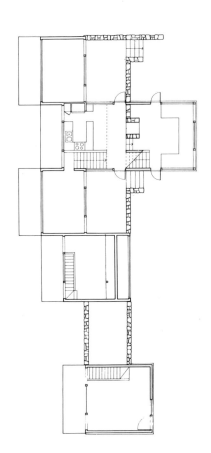

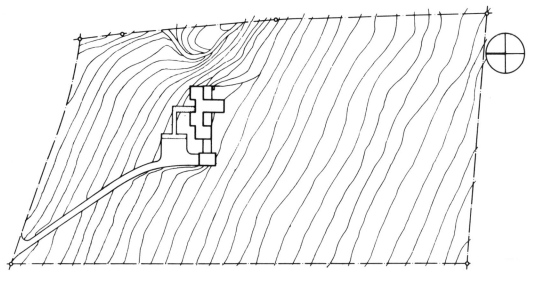

Left: *The house opens up to generous views downslope to the north, permitting broad prospects of the property as it rambles through fields and woods (Top). On the south side of the house, terraces and open exterior living spaces extend into the landscape. These "outdoor rooms" encourage an easy flow of space between exterior and interior (Bottom).*

Opposite Page: *As it faces north, the house opens up to views downhill.*
The natural wood siding helps to blend the house into the landscape.

Right: *A massive fieldstone fireplace dominates the living space.*

Opposite Page: *A view from the third level down toward the living room.*

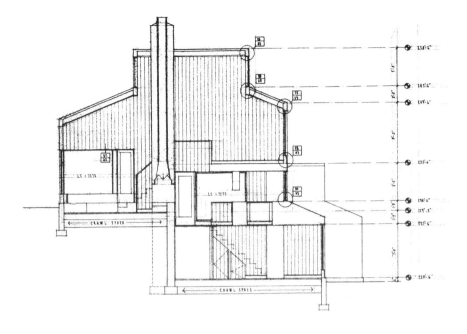

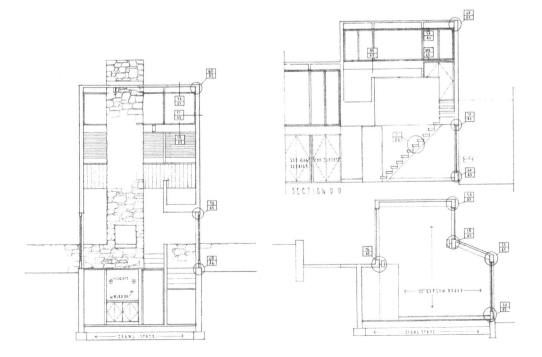

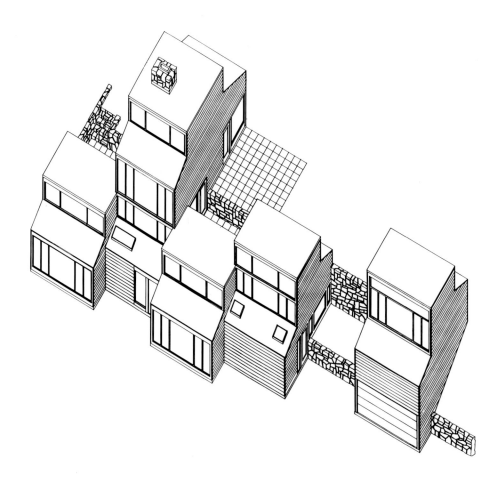

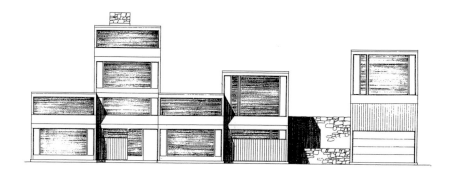

Left: *The children's room is a double-height space with abundant natural light.*

Opposite Page: *The kitchen/dining area is the very heart of the house. Photo: Bill Maris. Natural wood walls are a feature throughout the house, even in the bathrooms.*

De Vido House

East Hampton, New York

This country house for the architect and his family is a work in progress, having been added to and modified since it was first constructed. The basic design concept of natural wood, exposed structure, and natural light is preserved throughout.

The rooms are arranged around a great two-story living space, transparent at both ends, with views to the woods. A gallery, above the living room at the second story, leads to two bedrooms and a bathroom. There are stairs to a pair of third-story hideaway spaces. Additions include bedrooms and baths on the first floor and skylights to enhance natural illumination.

The house celebrates its sturdy timber construction. The Douglas fir structural frame, combined with two pairs of central columns and an X-truss, is faced indoors with rough-sawn cedar walls and polished white pine floors. The exterior is clad with cedar shingles and features dark window and door trim.

Besides the house and its additions and outbuildings, the landscape has been the object of much attention. Water is incorporated in several locations, ranging from a large angular pond to a small four-by-six-foot pool. Outdoor rooms, such as a gazebo, extend the house into the landscape through the use of wood fences weaving through the white pine forest.

SIDE ELEVATIONS

FRONT ELEVATION

REAR ELEVATION

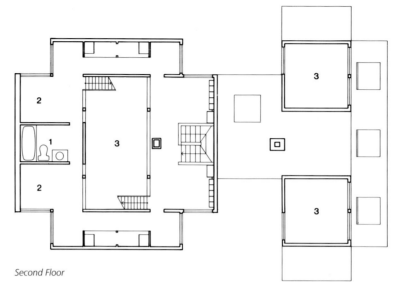

Second Floor

1. Bathroom
2. Bedroom
3. Open to below

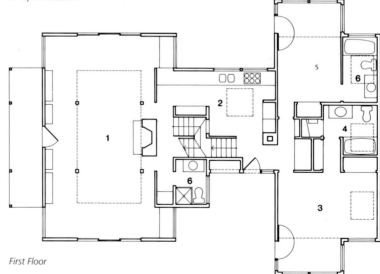

First Floor

1. Living Room
2. Kitchen
3. Bedroom
4. Bathroom
5. Bedroom
6. Bathroom

2   5   10

Left: *The house is surrounded by landscape and water features. Landscaping and water has been treated in a natural state around the house.*

Opposite Page: *The core of the house is a living space surrounded by bedrooms on the upper floors.*

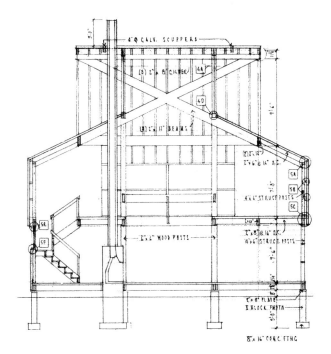

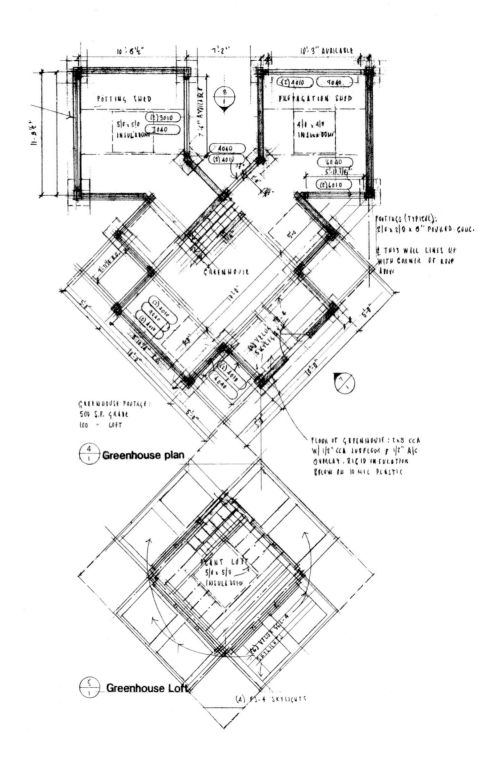

POTTING SHED

PROPAGATION SHED

GREENHOUSE

FOOTINGS (TYPICAL):
2'0 x 2'0 x 8" POURED CONC.

& THIS WALL LINES UP
WITH CORNER OF ROOF
ABOVE

GREENHOUSE FOOTAGE:
500 S.F. GRADE
100 " LOFT

FLOOR OF GREENHOUSE: 2x8 CCA
W/ 1/2" CCA SUBFLOOR & 1/2" A/C
OVERLAY, RIGID INSULATION
BELOW ON 10 MIL PLASTIC

$\frac{4}{1}$ **Greenhouse plan**

PLANT LOFT

$\frac{5}{1}$ **Greenhouse Loft**

(A) FS-4 SKYLIGHTS

Left: *Walls throughout the house are left as natural wood, warmed by the sun.*

Opposite Page: *Rooms are filled with natural light and warm natural materials. Tight spaces have built-in storage and ship-like coziness.*

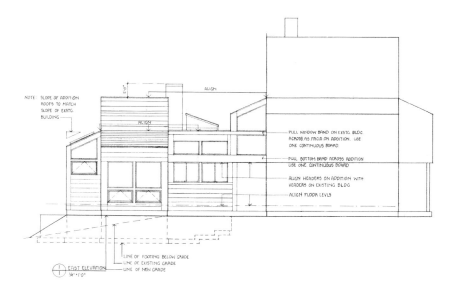

NOTE: SLOPE OF ADDITION ROOFS TO MATCH SLOPE OF EXSTG. BUILDING

ALIGN

ALIGN

PULL WINDOW BAND ON EXSTG. BLDG. ACROSS AS FACIA ON ADDITION. USE ONE CONTINUOUS BOARD.

PULL BOTTOM BAND ACROSS ADDITION USE ONE CONTINUOUS BOARD

ALIGN HEADERS ON ADDITION WITH HEADERS ON EXISTING BLDG

ALIGN FLOOR LEVLS

LINE OF FOOTING BELOW GRADE
LINE OF EXISTING GRADE
LINE OF NEW GRADE

1 EAST ELEVATION
   1/4" = 1'0"

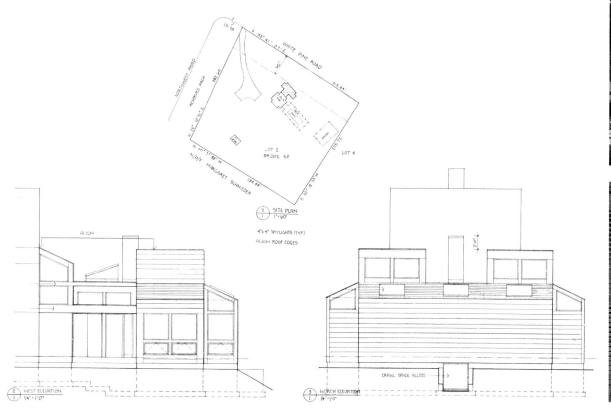

9 SITE PLAN
   1" = 60'

ALIGN

4"x4" SKYLIGHTS (TYP)
ALIGN ROOF EDGES

CRAWL SPACE ACCESS

2 WEST ELEVATION
   1/4" = 1'0"

9 NORTH ELEVATION
   1/4" = 1'0"

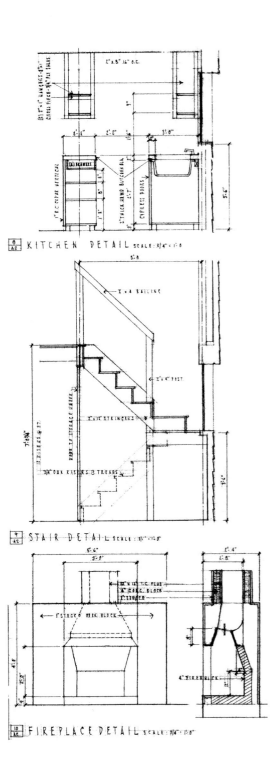

Right: *A corner in the master bedroom reveals the warmth of wood-clad interior. The bedrooms exude a cabin-like quality with high spaces and lots of natural light.*

Opposite Page: *The core of the house is a multi-story living space with views from a second floor gallery.*

Connecticut Hilltop House

Lakeville, Connecticut

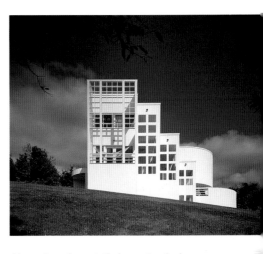

To capture a lake view and achieve solar benefits at the same time, this house features large glass areas facing south. The glass walls step back and up so that sunlight can penetrate to rooms on the north side of the house and allow these spaces to benefit from the view as well.

The house perches on the site like a sculptural assemblage, its white-painted vertical wood siding modeling curved surfaces and lending a variegated texture.

An entry on the uphill side of the house provides access to the main living area. From the foyer, one steps down into the faceted living room space, with its stepped window wall. On the foyer level, a library overlooks the living room. The dining space occupies its own glassy pavilion near the black-lacquered open-plan kitchen. The strong curved element on the first floor contains an open deck off the living room and dining room.

The master bedroom and a guest bedroom hover above this main floor, opening to the two-story space to gain views and sunlight. The rooftop contains a skylit studio spaced with commanding vistas to the south. The lower level contains guest rooms and recreation areas.

Above: From the west, the house steps back and opens in a sundeck that filters light.

Opposite Page: In contrast to its green landscape site, the house appears as a pristine sculptural object.

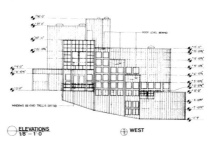

SOUTH   ELEVATIONS
         1/8" = 1'-0"   WEST

Roof Studio

1. *Studio*
2. *Roof Deck*

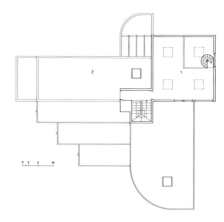

Second Floor

1. *Master Bedroom*
2. *Lower Studio*
3. *Bath*
4. *Open*
5. *Bedroom*

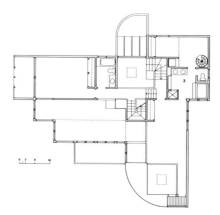

First Floor

1. *Entry*
2. *Living Room*
3. *Library*
4. *Garage*
5. *Powder Room*
6. *Kitchen*
7. *Dining*

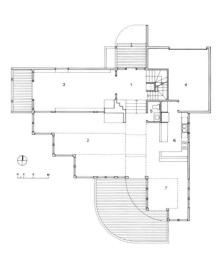

Left: *The entry vestibule is a two-story space with large windows to capture north light.*

Opposite Page: *From the south, the house surmounts the site and its grassy knoll. The north elevation contains the main entry and has textured wood siding.*

Right: *The living room, looking toward the kitchen and dining pavilion, has light from overhead. The volume of this space is dramatically modeled as the ceiling steps back in a series of "trays" and is overlooked by balconies above.*

Opposite Page: *Gridded planes of windows step out toward the landscape, capturing views of the surrounding countryside. The gridded nature of the wall gives these large planes scale and a structural rigor.*

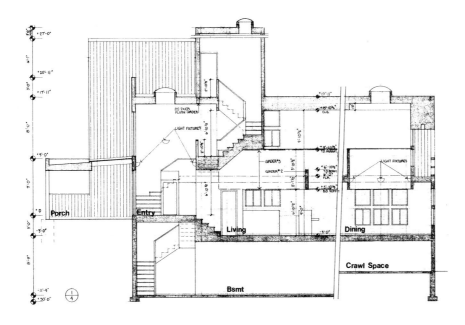

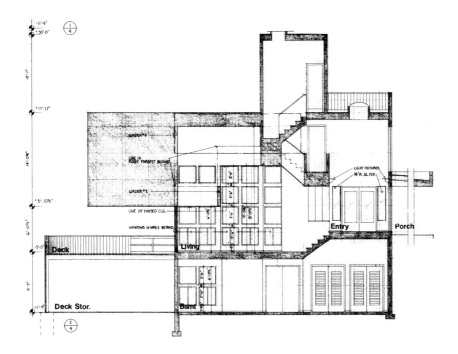

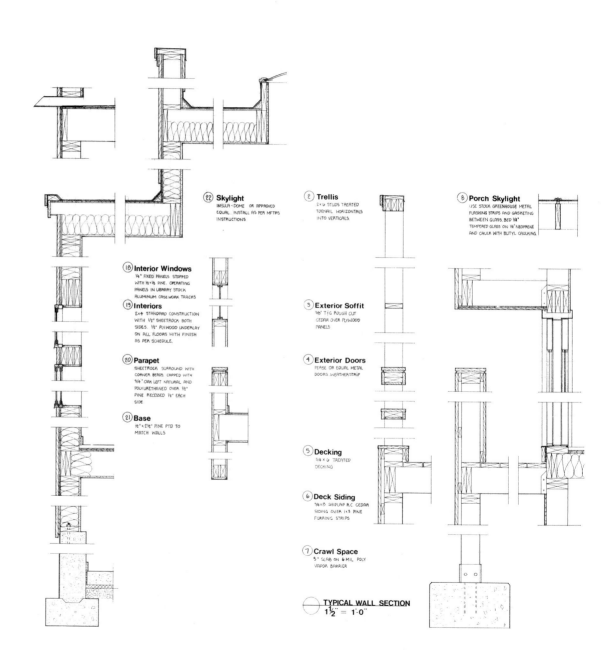

22 Skylight
INSULA-DOME OR APPROVED EQUAL. INSTALL AS PER MFTRS INSTRUCTIONS

18 Interior Windows
1/4" FIXED PANELS STOPPED WITH 1/2×1/2 PINE. OPERATING PANELS IN LIBRARY STOCK ALUMINUM CASEWORK TRACKS

19 Interiors
2×4 STANDARD CONSTRUCTION WITH 1/2" SHEETROCK BOTH SIDES. 1/2" PLYWOOD UNDERLAY ON ALL FLOORS WITH FINISH AS PER SCHEDULE.

20 Parapet
SHEETROCK SURROUND WITH CORNER BEADS. CAPPED WITH 3/4" OAK LEFT NATURAL AND POLYURETHANED OVER 1/2" PINE RECESSED 1/2" EACH SIDE

21 Base
1/2"×2 1/2" PINE PTD TO MATCH WALLS

2 Trellis
2×6 STUDS TREATED TOENAIL HORIZONTALS INTO VERTICALS

3 Exterior Soffit
3/8" T&G ROUGH CUT CEDAR OVER PLYWOOD PANELS

4 Exterior Doors
PEASE OR EQUAL METAL DOORS. WEATHERSTRIP

5 Decking
5/4 × 6 TREATED DECKING

6 Deck Siding
3/4×8 SHIPLAP R.C CEDAR SIDING OVER 1×3 PINE FURRING STRIPS

7 Crawl Space
5" SLAB ON 6 MIL POLY VAPOR BARRIER

8 Porch Skylight
USE STOCK GREENHOUSE METAL FLASHING STRIPS AND GASKETING BETWEEN GLASS. BED 1/4" TEMPERED GLASS ON 1/8" NEOPRENE AND CAULK WITH BUTYL CAULKING.

TYPICAL WALL SECTION
1 1/2" = 1'-0"

Wright House

Guilford, Connecticut

T he design of this house in the Connecticut hills employs simple geometric forms to suggest the elemental concept of shelter, while also recalling the shapes of ships and sails. Large windows throughout the living areas maximize views.

The various geometric elements are also emphasized by means of color. For example, the roof and gable end are separated from the walls below by a band of recessed windows. This band is stained in a gray color darker than that of the walls below and that of the light gable ends of the roof structure. The same idea is used in the color and separation of the chimney mass from the house and also in the curved "add-ons" to the simple rectangular form of the house.

A similar approach to color is found inside. Here, colors are applied in layers, such as in the gray layered grid on a yellow background that in turn overlays the window pattern. The wall is capped by another color band encasing the high windows. A gently curving glass-block wall offers light with privacy on the approach side of the house.

The furniture in the living room and the banquette in the sitting room were designed by the architects. The forms are upholstered and soft, in contrast to the geometry of the walls.

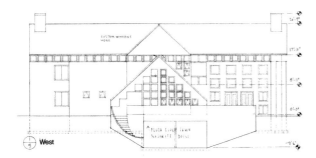

West

1. Bedroom
2. Master Bedroom
3. Master Bath
4. Landing
5. Study
6. Bath
7. Laundry Room

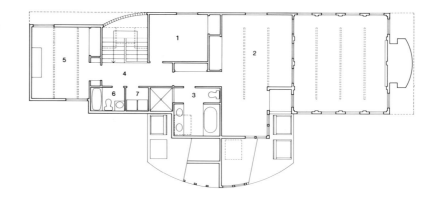

SECOND FLOOR PLAN

1. Lobby
2. Entry
3. Study
4. Dining Room
5. Kitchen
6. Family Room
7. Living Room
8. Powder Room

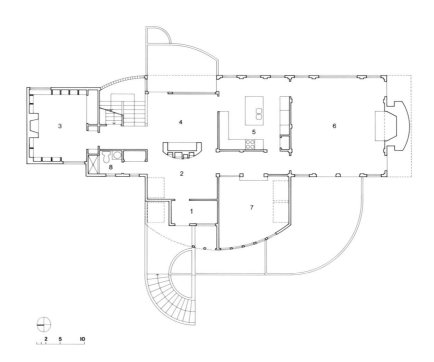

2 5 10

FIRST FLOOR PLAN

Left: *The south end of the house has a magnified scale with bold geometric forms.*

Opposite Page: *The approach side of the house features a gently arched glass block wall. A wide, generous stairway receives natural light through the glass block wall.*

Right: Detail of the west wall, behind which is the living room.

Opposite Page: A niche wall at the entry displays a portion of the owners' art collection. Views to the west from the living room, with French doors to the terrace.

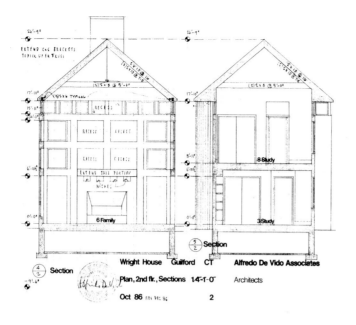

Wright House   Guilford   CT   **Alfredo De Vido Associates**

Plan, 2nd flr., Sections 1/4"=1'-0"   Architects

Oct 86   2

Section

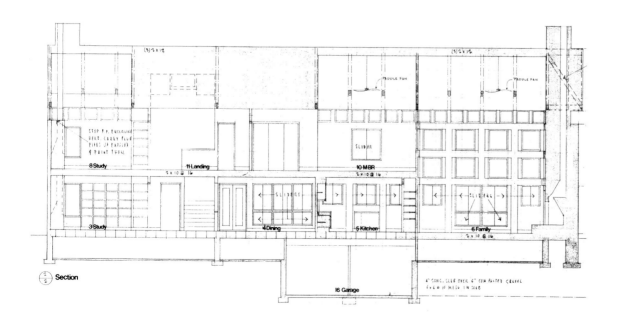

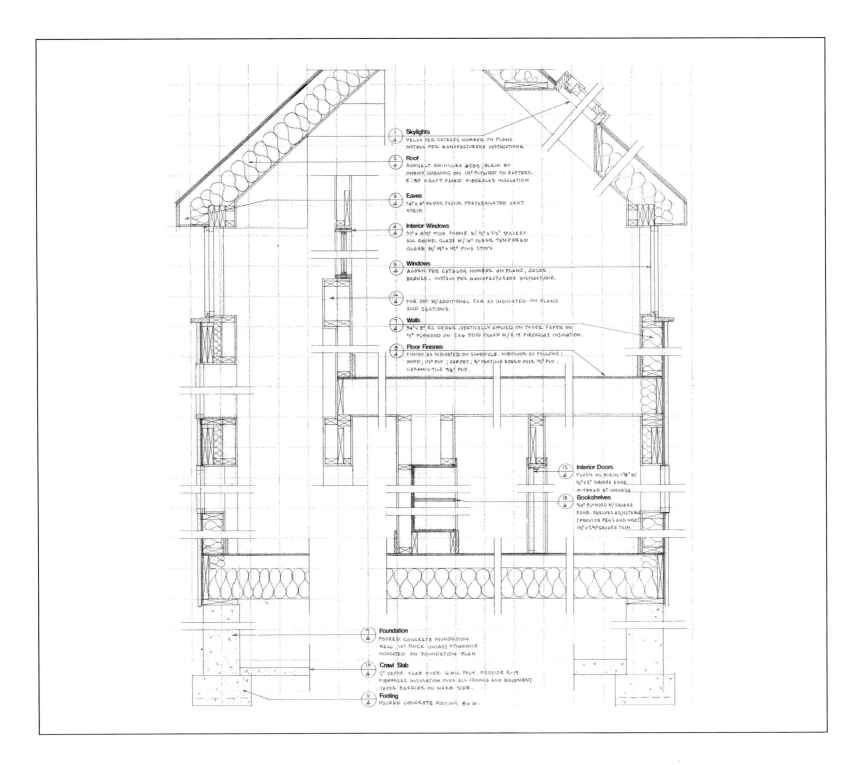

1/4 Skylights
VELUX PER CATALOG NUMBER ON PLANS.
INSTALL PER MANUFACTURER'S INSTRUCTIONS.

2/4 Roof
ASPHALT SHINGLES #235, BLACK BY
OWENS CORNING ON 1/2" PLYWOOD ON RAFTERS.
R-30 KRAFT FACED FIBERGLAS INSULATION

3/4 Eaves
3/4" X 6" CEDAR FASCIA. PREFABRICATED VENT
STRIP.

4/4 Interior Windows
3/4" X 4 1/2" PINE FRAME W/ 1/2" X 7 1/2" SPACERS.
ALL ROUND, GLAZE W/ 1/4" CLEAR TEMPERED
GLASS W/ 1/2" X 1/2" PINE STOPS.

5/4 Windows
ACORN PER CATALOG NUMBER ON PLANS, COLOR:
BRONZE - INSTALL PER MANUFACTURER'S INSTRUCTIONS.

6/4
FUR OUT W/ ADDITIONAL 2 X 4 AS INDICATED ON PLANS
AND SECTIONS.

7/4 Walls
3/4" X 8" RC CEDAR, VERTICALLY APPLIED ON TYVEK PAPER ON
1/2" PLYWOOD ON 2 X 6 STUD FILLED W/ R-19 FIBERGLAS INSULATION.

8/4 Floor Finishes
FINISH AS INDICATED ON SCHEDULE. SUBFLOOR AS FOLLOWS:
WOOD, 1/2" PLY; CARPET, 1/2" PARTICLE BOARD OVER 1/2" PLY,
CERAMIC TILE 5/8" PLY.

12/4 Interior Doors
FLUSH HC BIRCH 1 3/8" W/
1/2" X 2" SQUARE EDGE
MITERED AT CORNERS.

13/4 Bookshelves
3/4" PLYWOOD W/ SQUARE
EDGE. SHELVES ADJUSTABLE
(PROVIDE PEGS AND HOLES)
1/2" X 2 1/2" SQUARE TRIM.

9/4 Foundation
POURED CONCRETE FOUNDATION
WALL, 10" THICK UNLESS OTHERWISE
INDICATED ON FOUNDATION PLAN

10/4 Crawl Slab
2" VAPOR SLAB OVER 6 MIL POLY. PROVIDE R-19
FIBERGLAS INSULATION OVER ALL CRAWLS AND BASEMENT
VAPOR BARRIER ON WARM SIDE.

11/4 Footing
POURED CONCRETE FOOTING 8 X 16.

Right: *The living room features a wall dominated by a fireplace and layered with color.*

Opposite Page: *The window walls are composed of highly articulated openings which suggest the building's structure, and serve to break down the scale of this space.*

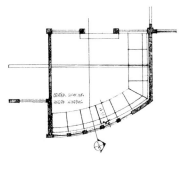

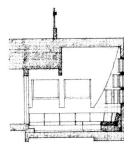

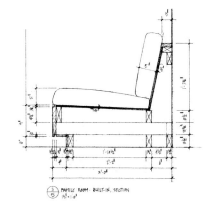

1 — FAMILY ROOM: PLAN

2 — FAMILY ROOM: SECTION

3 — FAMILY ROOM: BUILT-IN, SECTION

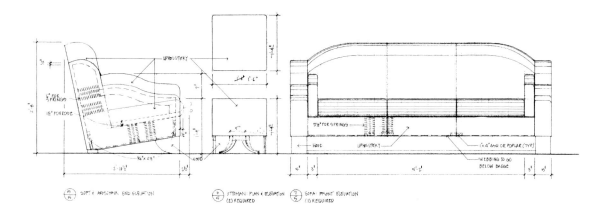

5 — SOFA & ARMCHAIR, END ELEVATION

6 — OTTOMAN: PLAN & ELEVATION
(2) REQUIRED

7 — SOFA: FRONT ELEVATION
(1) REQUIRED

8 — SOFA: PLAN

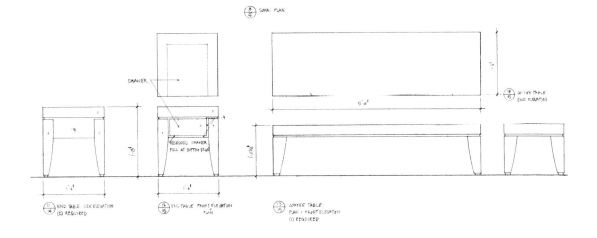

11 — END TABLE SIDE ELEVATION
(2) REQUIRED

12 — END TABLE FRONT ELEVATION
PLAN

13 — COFFEE TABLE:
PLAN & FRONT ELEVATION
(1) REQUIRED

14 — COFFEE TABLE
END ELEVATION

Quinones/Bieganek House

East Hampton, New York

B old color, strong forms, and soaring spaces distinguish this house with views over freshwater wetlands. The house's proximity to the water, however, complicated its design. Wetlands restrictions on the three-acre (1.2 hectare) woodland site reduced buildable area to less than a quarter of an acre (a tenth of a hectare). The balance of the property was to be deeded to the town as an scenic area to conserve the natural beauty of the land.

After the complex set of approvals was complete, and budget and program requirements set, construction began. The design consists of two rectangular blocks, joined by a diagonal connection that penetrates the entire house to form porches and decks to the northeast and southwest. Peaked roofs were set apart by means of changes in material from shingles to copper roofing at the center of the composition. Red-painted panels set against black-stained cedar dramatizes the modular system on the outside.

Inside the house, surprise vistas are revealed by the diagonal intersection of the basic rectangular forms. A bold, round column at the entrance serves as a hinge between foyer and living spaces. The living and dining room furniture, designed by the architect, is an elaboration on the house's overall design concept.

Above: *From the northeast, the house offers a sheltered entry defined by two wings.*

Opposite Page: *The bold use of color helps to break down the scale of the house.*

1. *Master Bedroom*
2. *Master Bath*
3. *Bath*
4. *Bedroom*

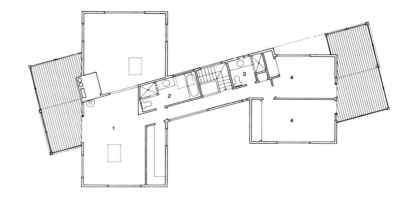

SECOND FLOOR PLAN

1. *Entry*
2. *Living Room*
3. *Dining Room*
4. *Kitchen*
5. *Powder Room*
6. *Garage*
7. *Laundry*

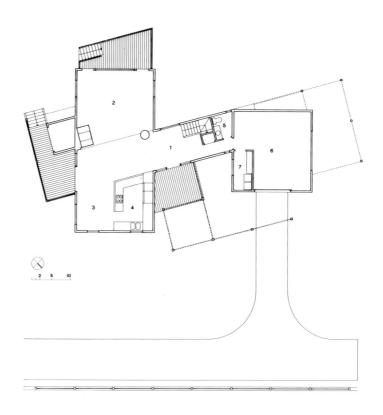

FIRST FLOOR PLAN

Left: *Living area is contained within a soaring two-story space, dominated by large windows opening to views of the surrounding landscape. Variegated ceiling surfaces add drama to this room.*

Opposite Page: *The bold, red gabled elements are clearly differentiated from the black-painted cross wings. From the southeast, the house reveals the gabled form that extends from end to end.*

Right: *View from the living area to the dining area reveals the illuminated ceiling volume that dominates this space. The strong form of the fireplace provides a visual anchor.*

Opposite Page: *The canopy of the bed becomes an integral part of the design.*

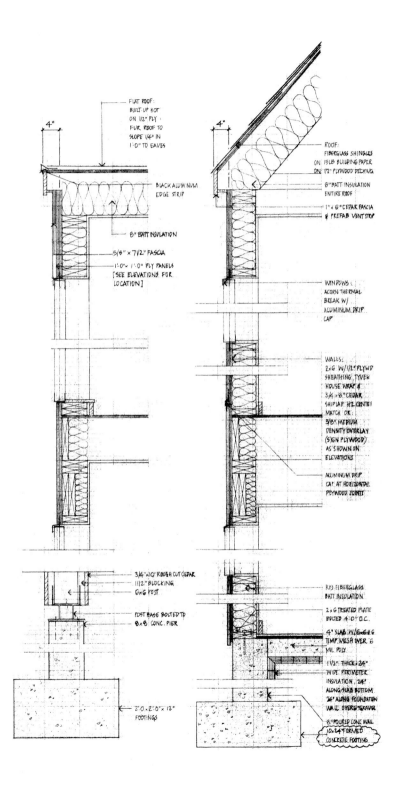

FLAT ROOF:
BUILT UP HOT
ON 1/2" PLY:
FUR ROOF TO
SLOPE 1/4" IN
1'-0" TO EAVES

BLACK ALUMINUM
EDGE STRIP

8" BATT INSULATION

5/8" × 7 1/2" FASCIA

1'-0"× 1'-0" PLY PANELS
[SEE ELEVATIONS FOR
LOCATION]

3/4"×10" ROUGH CUT CEDAR

1 1/2" BLOCKING

6×6 POST

POST BASE BOLTED TO
8×8 CONC. PIER

2'-0"× 2'-0"× 12"
FOOTINGS

ROOF:
FIBERGLASS SHINGLES
ON 15 LB BUILDING PAPER
ON 1/2" PLYWOOD DECKING

8" BATT INSULATION
ENTIRE ROOF

1"× 6" CEDAR FASCIA
& PREFAB VENT STRIP

WINDOWS:
ACORN THERMAL
BREAK W/
ALUMINUM DRIP
CAP

WALLS:
2×6 W/1/2" PLYWD
SHEATHING, TYVEK
HOUSE WRAP &
3/4 ×6" CEDAR
SHIPLAP #2 CENTER
MATCH OR
5/8" MEDIUM
DENSITY OVERLAY
(SIGN PLYWOOD)
AS SHOWN ON
ELEVATIONS

ALUMINUM DRIP
CAP AT HORIZONTAL
PLYWOOD JOINTS

R11 FIBERGLASS
BATT INSULATION

2×6 TREATED PLATE
BOLTED 4'-0" O.C.

4" SLAB W/6×6 #6
TEMP MESA OVER 6
MIL POLY

1 1/2" THICK×24"
WIDE PERIMETER
INSULATION, 24"
ALONG SLAB BOTTOM
24" ALONG FOUNDATION
WALL OVER 6" GRAVEL

8" POURED CONC WALL
10×24 FORMED
CONCRETE FOOTING

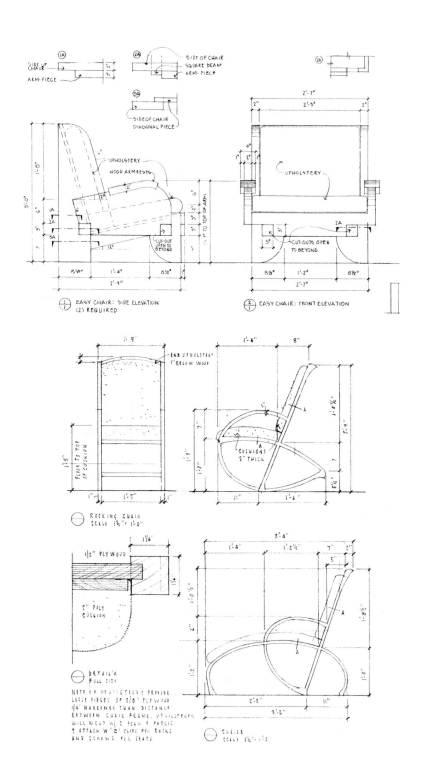

SIDE OF CHAIR
ARM-PIECE

SIDE OF CHAIR
SQUARE BEAM
ARM-PIECE

SIDE OF CHAIR
DIAGONAL PIECE

UPHOLSTERY
WOOD ARMRESTS

UPHOLSTERY

CUT-OUT OPEN TO BEYOND

CUT-OUTS OPEN TO BEYOND

EASY CHAIR: SIDE ELEVATION
(2) REQUIRED

EASY CHAIR: FRONT ELEVATION

END UPHOLSTERY
1" BELOW WOOD

CUSHIONS
3" THICK

FLOOR TO TOP OF CUSHION

ROCKING CHAIR
SCALE 1¼" = 1'-0"

1/2" PLYWOOD

2" POLY
CUSHION

DETAIL 'A
FULL SIZE

NOTE RE UPHOLSTERY: PROVIDE
LOOSE PIECES OF 3/8" PLYWOOD
1/4" NARROWER THAN DISTANCE
BETWEEN CHAIR FRAME. UPHOLSTERY
WILL WRAP W/ 3" FOAM & FABRIC
& ATTACH W/ 2" CLIPS FOR BACKS
AND SCREWS FOR SEATS

CHAISE
SCALE 1½" = 1'-0"

Left: *Specially designed furniture, such as this piece in the master bedroom, is found throughout the house.*

Opposite Page: *The architect's design of a rocker and a chaise reflect a lightness of touch and an elegance of detail, appropriate to the house's architecture.*

New Preston House

New Preston, Connecticutt

R esponding to the owner's request for a house on a ten-acre (four-hectare) site in harmony with northwestern Connecticut's rural landscape, De Vido took New England's vernacular architecture—particularly the salt box house—as his inspiration for the exterior design. A combination of square windows, screens, and light gray cedar siding give the exterior of this house its lacy, open quality.

Inside, the 3,082-square-foot (277-square-meter) house is a collection of open, light-filled spaces. The main entrance is a connected structure, built on an axis of the house between a guest wing and a large garage. A barn completes the grouping. The glassy vestibule extends out to the visitor in welcome.

The plan has the faceted quality of a diamond. Interior walls are skewed, providing a series of vistas through the major rooms. A central, two-sided fieldstone chimney is viewed from both the entrance and the living room. The walls are trimmed with bands and pilasters of bleached pine.

From the vestibule, one enters the large, unbroken space of the living room. Flanking this space to the east is a light-filled dining pavilion, while to the west is the master bedroom. All of these spaces open up with sweeping views of a lake to the north.

Above: *A view from the northwest reveals the slat-box from inspired by vernacular architecture.*

Opposite Page: *Viewed through the fence that defines the entry court, the vestibule extends out.*

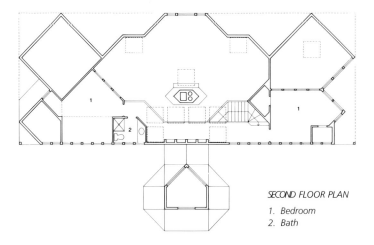

SECOND FLOOR PLAN

1. *Bedroom*
2. *Bath*

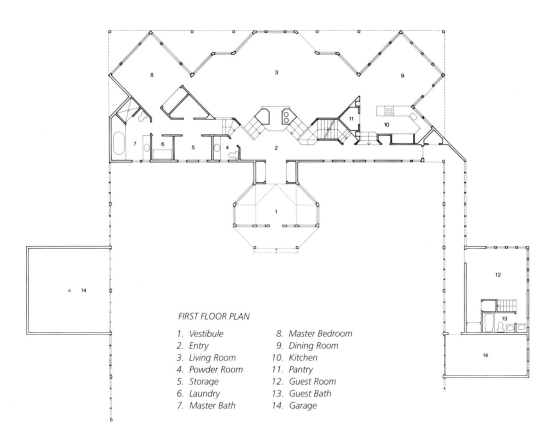

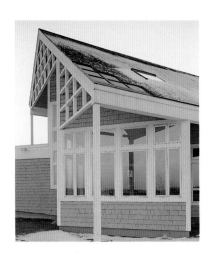

FIRST FLOOR PLAN

1. *Vestibule*	8. *Master Bedroom*
2. *Entry*	9. *Dining Room*
3. *Living Room*	10. *Kitchen*
4. *Powder Room*	11. *Pantry*
5. *Storage*	12. *Guest Room*
6. *Laundry*	13. *Guest Bath*
7. *Master Bath*	14. *Garage*

Right: *From the southeast, the house has a variegated form and sheltering nooks. From the south, the house welcomes visitors with a gem-like vestibule.*

Opposite Page: *Working drawings of the wall sections are condensed to communicate a great deal of construction information on a single sheet.*

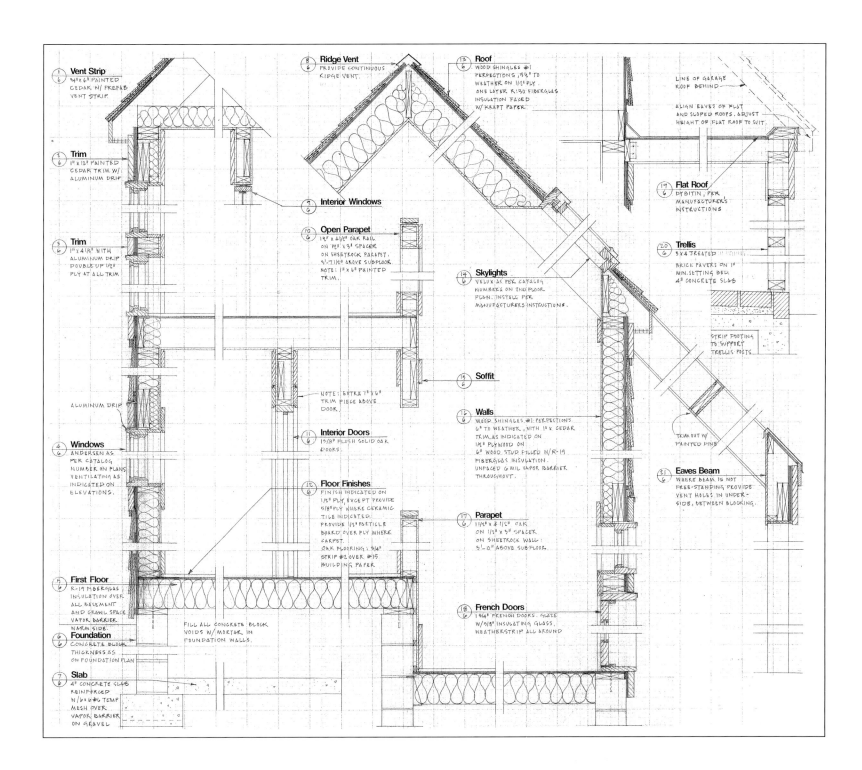

1/6 Vent Strip
3/4" x 6" PAINTED CEDAR W/ PREFAB VENT STRIP.

2/6 Trim
1" x 12" PAINTED CEDAR TRIM W/ ALUMINUM DRIP

3/6 Trim
1" x 4 1/2" WITH ALUMINUM DRIP DOUBLE UP 1/2" PLY AT ALL TRIM

ALUMINUM DRIP

4/6 Windows
ANDERSEN AS PER CATALOG NUMBER ON PLANS VENTILATING AS INDICATED ON ELEVATIONS.

5/6 First Floor
R-19 FIBERGLAS INSULATION OVER ALL BASEMENT AND CRAWL SPACE VAPOR BARRIER WARM SIDE.

6/6 Foundation
CONCRETE BLOCK THICKNESS AS ON FOUNDATION PLAN

7/6 Slab
4" CONCRETE SLAB REINFORCED W/ 6x6 #6 TEMP MESH OVER VAPOR BARRIER ON GRAVEL

8/6 Ridge Vent
PROVIDE CONTINUOUS RIDGE VENT.

9/6 Interior Windows

10/6 Open Parapet
1 1/2" x 4 1/2" OAK RAIL ON 1/2" x 3" SPACER ON SHEETROCK PARAPET. 3'-7 1/2" ABOVE SUBFLOOR. NOTE: 1" x 6" PAINTED TRIM.

NOTE: EXTRA 1" x 6" TRIM PIECE ABOVE DOOR.

11/6 Interior Doors
1 3/8" FLUSH SOLID OAK DOORS.

12/6 Floor Finishes
FINISH INDICATED ON 1/2" PLY, EXCEPT PROVIDE 5/8" PLY WHERE CERAMIC TILE INDICATED. PROVIDE 1/2" PARTICLE BOARD OVER PLY WHERE CARPET. OAK FLOORING; 3/4" STRIP #2 OVER #15 BUILDING PAPER.

FILL ALL CONCRETE BLOCK VOIDS W/ MORTAR IN FOUNDATION WALLS.

13/6 Roof
WOOD SHINGLES #1 PERFECTIONS; 5 1/2" TO WEATHER ON 1/2" PLY. ONE LAYER R-30 FIBERGLAS INSULATION FACED W/ KRAFT PAPER.

14/6 Skylights
VELUX AS PER CATALOG NUMBERS ON 2ND FLOOR PLAN. INSTALL PER MANUFACTURERS INSTRUCTIONS.

15/6 Soffit

16/6 Walls
WOOD SHINGLES #1 PERFECTIONS 6" TO WEATHER, WITH 1" x CEDAR TRIM AS INDICATED ON 1/2" PLYWOOD ON 6" WOOD STUD FILLED W/R-19 FIBERGLAS INSULATION. UNFACED 6 MIL VAPOR BARRIER THROUGHOUT.

17/6 Parapet
1 1/2" x 4 1/2" OAK ON 1/2" x 3" SPACER ON SHEETROCK WALL. 3'-0" ABOVE SUBFLOOR.

18/6 French Doors
1 3/4" FRENCH DOORS. GLAZE W/ 5/8" INSULATING GLASS, WEATHERSTRIP ALL AROUND

LINE OF GARAGE ROOF BEHIND

ALIGN EAVES OF FLAT AND SLOPED ROOFS. ADJUST HEIGHT OF FLAT ROOF TO SUIT.

19/6 Flat Roof
DY-BITIN, PER MANUFACTURER'S INSTRUCTIONS

20/6 Trellis
3 x 4 TREATED BRICK PAVERS ON 1" MIN. SETTING BED. 4" CONCRETE SLAB

STRIP FOOTING TO SUPPORT TRELLIS POSTS

TRIM OUT W/ PAINTED PINE

21/6 Eaves Beam
WHERE BEAM IS NOT FREE-STANDING PROVIDE VENT HOLES IN UNDERSIDE, BETWEEN BLOCKING.

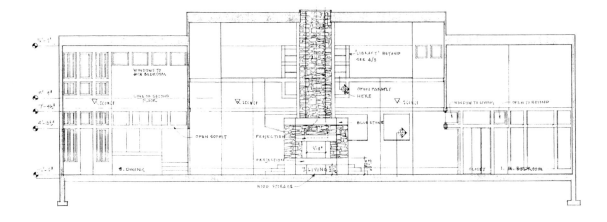

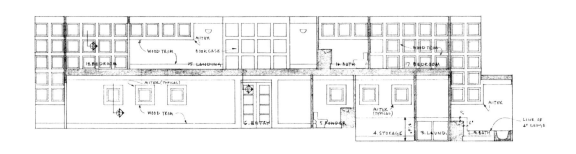

Left: *The living space is dominated by an imposing fireplace with its fieldstone chimney. Stairs to this space split around this masonry mass and deliver one to either side.*

Opposite Page: *Large square and rectangular cutouts and windows frame views of the countryside beyond the house, and also views from one space to another.*

Wertheimer House

Bethany Beach, Delaware

This octagonal house serves as a weekend/vacation retreat for a Washington, D.C. attorney and his family of six. The site is close to the ocean in a dense beach community. On the adjacent lot existed a long, high house that blocked views of the water. To the rear of the property was a prominent sand dune and oblique ocean views, and the major spaces are oriented in this direction.

The house is set on piles to guard against flooding. To avoid the awkward look of a house on stilts, the piles are surrounded with textured cedar plywood—the assembly encloses a garage and storage. The octagonal form suggests the form of a lighthouse. The textured plywood covering the lower level of the house is stained black to downplay the lower level as much as possible. This is reinforced by the landscaping, which was mounded in dune fashion and planted with indigenous materials.

The spaces of the house are organized around the large, high-ceilinged living spaces, which feature freestanding columns and a series of exposed beams for lateral bracing. Interior surfaces are clad in rough-cut cedar plywood panels, whitewashed to eliminate the color variance that normally occurs between one plywood sheet and the other.

A second-floor bed/sitting room opens onto the living room below by a series of interior shutters. This device provides privacy when required and visual openness at other times.

Opposite Page: *Within the context of the dune, the house recalls the image of a lighthouse.*

Above: *The extensive use of glass catches views in several directions.*

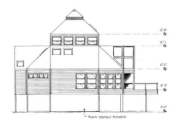

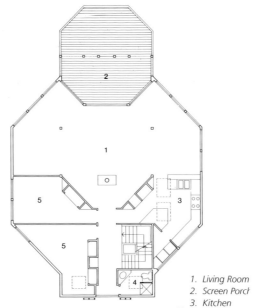

SECOND FLOOR PLAN

1. Living Room
2. Screen Porch
3. Kitchen
4. Bath
5. Bedroom

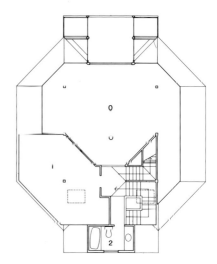

LOFT PLAN

1. Master Bedroom
2. Master Bath
3. Dressing

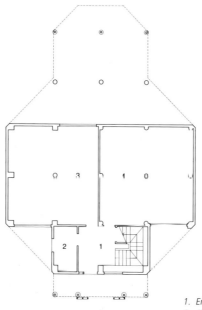

FIRST FLOOR PLAN

1. Entry
2. Shower
3. Storage
4. Garage

MEZZANINE PLAN

1. Bedroom
2. Bath
3. Open

Left: *The upper level offers dramatic, sweeping views of the maritime environment beyond. The space's interior communicates a sense of the house's structure.*

Opposite Page: *The south elevation overlooks water views framed by large openings. From the northwest, the house presents a restrained elevation, with minimal fenestration.*

Top: A view from the kitchen toward the glassy living area.

Bottom: Built-in counters and woodwork are finished in light colors to maximize lighting.

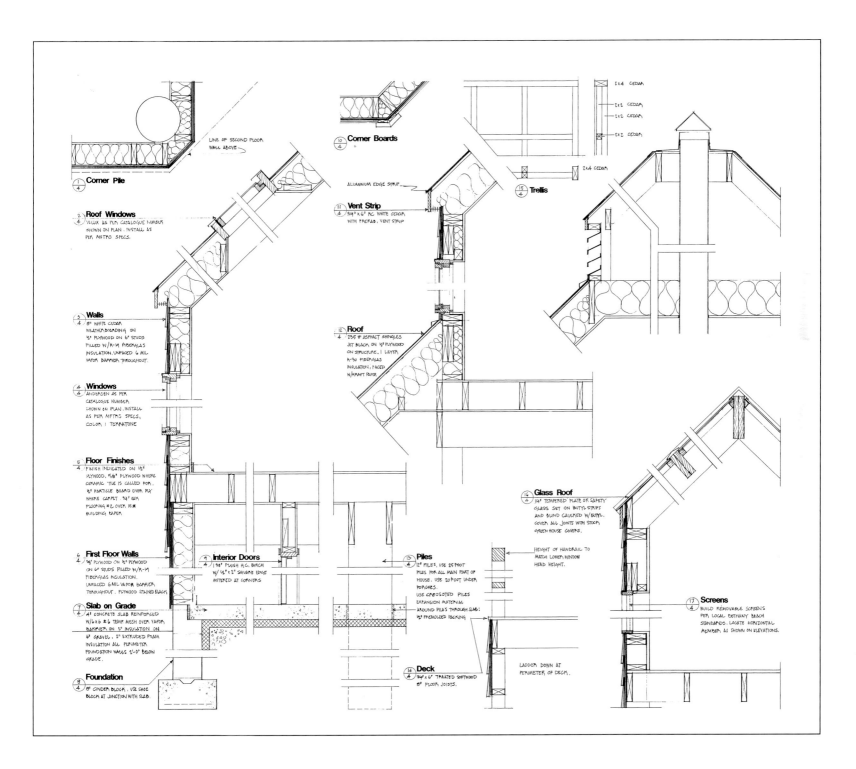

1 / 4 Corner Pile

LINE OF SECOND FLOOR
WALL ABOVE

2 / 4 Roof Windows
VELUX AS PER CATALOGUE NUMBER
SHOWN ON PLAN. INSTALL AS
PER MFTRS SPECS.

3 / 4 Walls
6" WHITE CEDAR
WEATHERBOARDING ON
½" PLYWOOD ON 6" STUDS
FILLED W/ R-19 FIBERGLAS
INSULATION, UNFACED 6 MIL
VAPOR BARRIER THROUGHOUT.

4 / 4 Windows
ANDERSEN AS PER
CATALOGUE NUMBER
SHOWN ON PLAN. INSTALL
AS PER MFTRS SPECS,
COLOR : TERRATONE

5 / 4 Floor Finishes
FINISH INDICATED ON ½"
PLYWOOD, ⅝" PLYWOOD WHERE
CERAMIC TILE IS CALLED FOR,
½" PARTICLE BOARD OVER PLY
WHERE CARPET. ¾" OAK
FLOORING #2 OVER 15#
BUILDING PAPER

6 / 4 First Floor Walls
⅝" PLYWOOD ON ½" PLYWOOD
ON 6" STUDS FILLED W/ R-19
FIBERGLAS INSULATION,
UNFACED 6 MIL VAPOR BARRIER
THROUGHOUT, PLYWOOD STAINED BLACK

7 / 4 Slab on Grade
4" CONCRETE SLAB REINFORCED
W/ 6 x 6 #6 TEMP. MESH OVER VAPOR
BARRIER ON 1" INSULATION ON
6" GRAVEL. 2" EXTRUDED FOAM
INSULATION ALL PERIMETER
FOUNDATION WALLS 2'-0" BELOW
GRADE.

8 / 4 Foundation
8" CINDER BLOCK, USE SHOE
BLOCK AT JUNCTION WITH SLAB.

9 / 4 Interior Doors
1¾" FLUSH H.C. BIRCH
W/ ½" x 1" SQUARE EDGE
MITERED AT CORNERS

10 / 4 Corner Boards

11 / 4 Vent Strip
¾" x 6" AC WHITE CEDAR
WITH PREFAB. VENT STRIP

ALUMINUM EDGE STRIP

12 / 4 Roof
235 # ASPHALT SHINGLES
JET BLACK ON ½" PLYWOOD
ON STRUCTURE, 1 LAYER
R-30 FIBERGLAS
INSULATION, FACED
W/ KRAFT PAPER

13 / 4 Piles
12" PILES, USE 25 FOOT
PILES FOR ALL MAIN PART OF
HOUSE. USE 20 FOOT UNDER
PORCHES.
USE CREOSOTED PILES
EXPANSION MATERIAL
AROUND PILES THROUGH SLAB:
½" PREMOLDED PACKING

14 / 4 Deck
¾" x 6" TREATED SOFTWOOD
8" FLOOR JOISTS.

2x4 CEDAR
2x2 CEDAR
2x2 CEDAR
2x2 CEDAR
2x4 CEDAR

15 / 4 Trellis

16 / 4 Glass Roof
¼" TEMPERED PLATE OR SAFETY
GLASS SET ON BUTYL STRIPS
AND BLIND CAULKED W/ BUTYL.
COVER ALL JOINTS WITH STOCK
GREEN HOUSE COVERS.

HEIGHT OF HANDRAIL TO
MATCH LOWER WINDOW
HEAD HEIGHT.

LADDER DOWN AT
PERIMETER OF DECK.

17 / 4 Screens
BUILD REMOVABLE SCREENS
PER LOCAL BETHANY BEACH
STANDARDS. LOCATE HORIZONTAL
MEMBER AS SHOWN ON ELEVATIONS.

$\frac{1}{5}$ **Section**

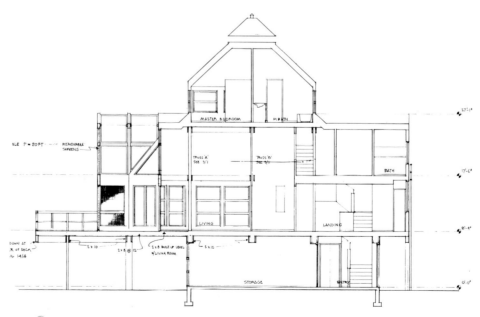

$\frac{2}{5}$ **Section**

Left: *The dining space is adjacent to the kitchen area, with its high ceiling and skylights.*

Opposite Page: *The master bedroom offers sweeping views and light from above. A stair up to the highest spaces is tucked into the octagonal roof.*

One White Pine Road House

East Hampton, New York

One at a time, Alfredo De Vido is designing and building all of the houses on White Pine Road, in East Hampton, Long Island, New York. The goal is a harmonious grouping with variety: certain simple geometric forms and natural materials are introduced and repeated, yet each house has an individual character.

This house is the eighth in the series. In its design it retains the gracious symmetry, triple gable, curving brackets, and natural cedar shingles characteristic of the east end of Long Island. The house is sited among tall trees that filter the sunlight and provide a canopy of green. To unify the exterior and to emphasize the various window openings and voids, distinctive bands of trim are painted dark green in contrast to the shingles.

Within the house, the shaping of space and detailing are contemporary, with crisp lines and open vistas. The plan features two sets of stairs to three bedrooms, two on either side of the living room, allowing flexibility of use and greater privacy in these areas. The bedrooms overlook the two-story living space, which opens to western views.

Above: *The front entry, facing east, welcomes visitors with a classically symmetrical facade.*

Opposite Page: *As it faces west, the back of the house opens to a terrace and views.*

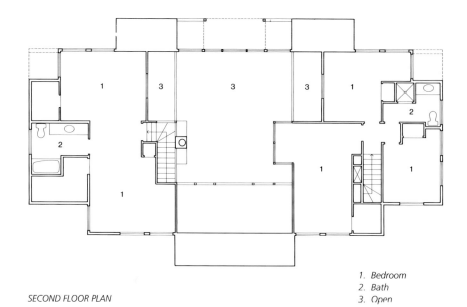

SECOND FLOOR PLAN

1. Bedroom
2. Bath
3. Open

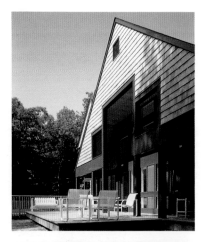

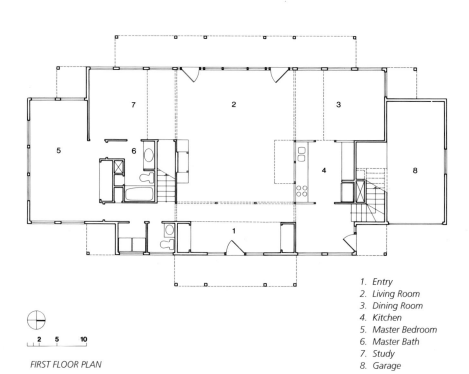

2   5   10

FIRST FLOOR PLAN

1. Entry
2. Living Room
3. Dining Room
4. Kitchen
5. Master Bedroom
6. Master Bath
7. Study
8. Garage

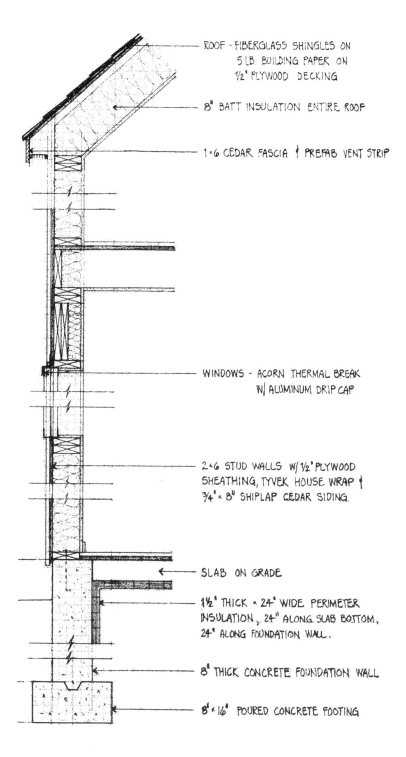

ROOF - FIBERGLASS SHINGLES ON
5 LB. BUILDING PAPER ON
½" PLYWOOD DECKING

8" BATT INSULATION ENTIRE ROOF

1×6 CEDAR FASCIA & PREFAB VENT STRIP

WINDOWS - ACORN THERMAL BREAK
W/ ALUMINUM DRIP CAP

2×6 STUD WALLS W/ ½" PLYWOOD
SHEATHING, TYVEK HOUSE WRAP &
¾" × 8" SHIPLAP CEDAR SIDING.

SLAB ON GRADE

1½" THICK × 24" WIDE PERIMETER
INSULATION, 24" ALONG SLAB BOTTOM,
24" ALONG FOUNDATION WALL.

8" THICK CONCRETE FOUNDATION WALL

8" × 16" POURED CONCRETE FOOTING

Drake House

Pound Ridge, New York

Sloping gently toward a lake, this site in a rural corner of New York is bounded by a cliff on one side and protected wetlands on the other. These site features limited the buildable area of the five-acre property. Other considerations affecting the house's design included the client's request for an indoor swimming pool, and the desire for as many rooms as possible to face toward the lake.

The design solution was to place the house's entry at mid-level on the hill, with other rooms stepping up and down from it via internal stairs, and with rooms nestled into the hillside. On the exterior, a palette of neutral stains accentuates the geometric variety, causing some forms to recede while others come to the fore.

At the house's center, space flows freely. Various spaces draw visual drama from their individual shapes, walls, and colonnades. Rooms are planned so that light floods in from a variety of directions while sweeping views are revealed. Since higher rooms overlook lower portions of the house, spaces were designed to provide visual interest when viewed from within.

On the lowest level is the indoor pool, contained by a space with an undulating wall that snakes toward the lake, fancifully suggesting a wave form to the water. A Brazilian wood ceiling complements the water's deep blue.

Above: *The exterior is a subtle composition of collaged geometric forms accented with color.*

Opposite Page: *Articulation of the house's various volumes breaks down the scale of the building and makes it more comprehensible.*

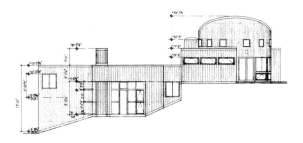

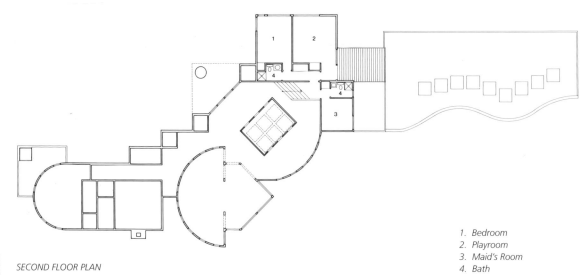

SECOND FLOOR PLAN

1. Bedroom
2. Playroom
3. Maid's Room
4. Bath

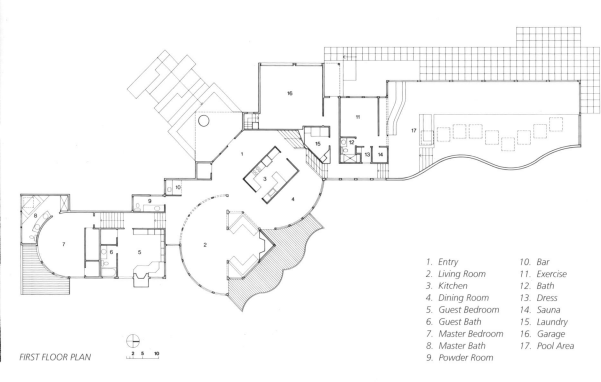

FIRST FLOOR PLAN

1. Entry
2. Living Room
3. Kitchen
4. Dining Room
5. Guest Bedroom
6. Guest Bath
7. Master Bedroom
8. Master Bath
9. Powder Room
10. Bar
11. Exercise
12. Bath
13. Dress
14. Sauna
15. Laundry
16. Garage
17. Pool Area

Right: The living area is found within a forest of columns and openings. As the fireplace provides a focus for the living room, circulation spaces allow one to move through the upper level, which offers views into these living realms.

Opposite Page: The pool's curved wall suggests not only the wave action of the water within this space, but also the lake which is just beyond the window wall.

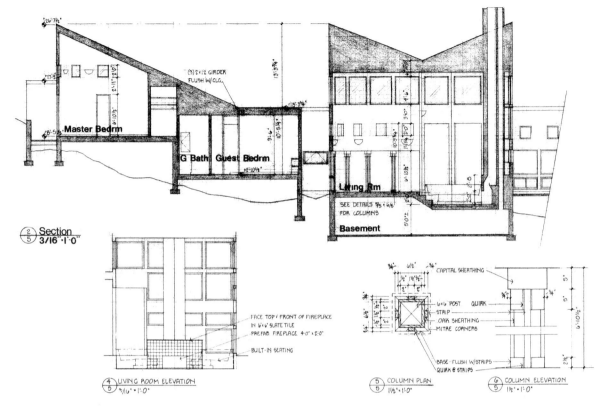

(3) 2×12 GIRDER FLUSH W/CLG.

Master Bedrm

G Bath **Guest Bedrm**

Living Rm

SEE DETAILS 5/5 & 6/5 FOR COLUMNS

Basement

2/5 **Section**
3/16"=1'-0"

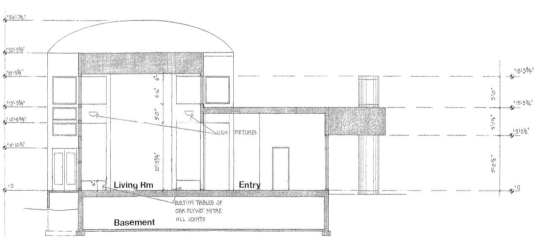

FACE TOP & FRONT OF FIREPLACE IN 6"×6" SLATE TILE
PREFAB FIREPLACE 4'-0"×2'-0"

BUILT-IN SEATING

4/5 **LIVING ROOM ELEVATION**
3/16" = 1'-0"

CAPITAL SHEATHING

6×6 POST   QUIRK
STRIP
OAK SHEATHING
MITRE CORNERS

BASE FLUSH W/STRIPS
QUIRK @ STRIPS

5/5 **COLUMN PLAN**
1½" = 1'-0"

6/5 **COLUMN ELEVATION**
1½" = 1'-0"

Living Rm   **Entry**

LIGHT FIXTURES

BUILT-IN TABLES OF OAK PLYWD MITRE ALL JOINTS

Basement

4/7 **Section**
3/16"=1'-0"

Wertheimer House	One White Pine Road House	Wright House	Drake House
Bethany Beach, Delaware	East Hampton, New York	Guilford, Connecticut	Pound Ridge, New York
Site: .25 acres (0.1 hectares)	Site: 2 acres (0.8 hectares)	Site: 3 acres (1.2 hectares)	Site: 5 acres (2 hectares)
Building: 2,500 sq. ft. (225 sq. mt.)	Building: 2,970 sq. ft. (267.3 sq. mt.)	Building: 2,960 sq. ft. (266.4 sq. mt.)	Building: 5,700 sq. ft. (513 sq. mt.)
Date of design: 1984	Date of design: 1987	Date of design: 1987	Date of design: 1987
Construction completed: 1985	Construction completed: 1987	Construction completed: 1988	Construction completed: 1988

Firm Profile

Alfredo De Vido, FAIA, holds a Bachelor of Architecture degree from Carnegie-Mellon University, a Master of Fine Arts from Princeton University, and a Diploma in Town Planning from the Royal Academy of Fine Arts, Copenhagen. At Carnegie-Mellon, De Vido received the American Institute of Architects Prize and the Pennsylvania Society of Architects Award.

While on active duty in the U.S. Navy "Seebees," De Vido was Officer in Charge of Construction and Design for the naval air station in Atsugi, Japan.

De Vido is a member of the American Institute of Architects College of Fellows, has served as a member and chairman of AIA committees and design award juries, and has lectured and taught at architecture schools throughout the U.S. and Canada. He has received design awards from national, state, and local AIA groups, *Architectural Record*, the U.S. Department of Housing and Urban Development, the City Club of New York, and other professional and trade organizations.

In addition to his practice, De Vido has authored a number of books, among them *Designing Your Client's House—An Architect's Guide to Meeting Design Goals and Budgets, Innovative Management Techniques for Architectural Design and Construction,* and *House Design: Art and Practice.*

The importance of achieving a high level of design quality while paying attention to the client's budget and schedule has led De Vido to an integrated organization of the design and construction phases. He combines this organization with a modular approach to all projects, including theaters, hotel/resort planning, schools, and store and office design, as well as to houses and housing.

Photographic Credits

James D'Addio

Quinones/Bieganek House

F. Charles Photography

One White Pine Road
Wright House

Robert Lautman

Foreword
Wertheimer House

Bill Maris

Wirth House

Norman McGrath

Introduction
De Vido House
Moore House
Quinones/Bieganek House

Paul Warchol

Connecticut Hilltop House
New Preston House
Quinones/Bieganek House
Drake House